Pat,
Enjoy + stay
encouraged! Kee
moving toward your
dreams!

Chanelle!

From My Heart to Your Soul

A Collection of Poetry To Encourage, Inspire and
Awaken YOUR Spirit

By Chanelle A. Watson

BLI Publishing
Dallas, TX

Chanelle A. Watson

Published by BLI Publishing, a subsidiary of The BLI Group, Dallas,
TX.

CreateSpace.

Printed in the United States of America.

Designed by BLI Solutions, a subsidiary of The BLI Group, Dallas, TX

All scriptures quotations, unless otherwise indicated, are taken from the
Holy Bible, various versions. All rights reserved.

ISBN: 0615987338
ISBN-13: 978-0615987330

DEDICATION

I'd like to dedicate this book to my family and those specific and special people God placed in my life to help me as I went through life's lessons. They were always there to encourage, inspire, keep me humbled and focused on what God had in store for me.

Because of God and their obedience to Him, my Spirit has been awakened.

"Love is patient and kind; love does not envy or boast; it is not arrogant or rude. It does not insist on its own way; it is not irritable or resentful; it does not rejoice at wrongdoing, but rejoices with the truth. Love bears all things, believes all things, hopes all things, endures all things. Love never ends. As for prophecies, they will pass away; as for tongues, they will cease; as for knowledge, it will pass away."

I Corinthians 13:4-8 ESV

TABLE OF CONTENTS

AUTHOR'S NOTE

Thank you to all of my loved ones and close friends who have supported me with everything I have done. From school graduations, to Chanelle's Heavenly Treasures, to all the moving around I have done. You have been there for me in spite of struggles, hesitations, or concerns. Your love truly has humbled me in so many ways and I thank God for placing you in my life to take this journey with me.

I've experienced my share of tough love that helped shape and guide me to a new beginning in my life. I have experienced my share of situations whether directly or indirectly that have changed me for the better. I thank God for these experiences, the people he has placed in my life for a time such as this, and I am blessed by the change that has moved from my heart to your eyes.

The collection of poems in this book are based on life lessons, life struggles, life accomplishments, that are not just mine but situations I have experienced, read or heard about.

All are a reflection of what the Holy Spirit has placed on my heart to share with you, the reader. Although, I do not have control over how anyone responds to certain poems or emotions that may arise from reading them, my genuine intention is to share my heart, my thoughts, and attempt to encourage or inspire you during the process.

This book is definitely close to my heart and I thank you for supporting it and my hope is that you enjoy it.

~ Chanelle

ACKNOWLEDGMENTS

First and foremost, I give ALL the glory to God for all the words, lines, and poems in this book. I thank Him for using me. I am truly blessed, thankful, highly favored, and grateful.

There are so many people to thank and acknowledge I am hesitant to call specific names because I do not want to forget anyone and how they have helped me along my journey thus far. If your name is not listed please charge it to my head and not my heart. Know that if we have interacted in any way that you have dropped bits and pieces of yourself into me and for that I appreciate and acknowledge you.

To my family, thank you for EVERYTHING! You all are truly a gift from God and there are not enough words or space to thank you for ALL you have instilled, changed, or helped me with over the years. I am so thankful to God for choosing you all to raise, minister, and humble me when I needed it the most. I love you all tremendously!

To Princess Williams, thank you for understanding me when no one else would. You truly are an amazing person and friend.

To my Sorors Adrienne Guillory and Carlita Wilson, thank you both for the talks we've had, they were always needed. Adrienne, thank you for being there that NYE, you were truly a lifesaver!!!

To Tisha McCormick, thank you for being there and opening your home to me. You were truly a blessing and I greatly appreciate you.

To my Shiloh family and Pastor Taylor thank you for teaching and getting me started on learning exactly who God is in my life.

To my KCC family and Pastor Goines, thank you for being there to help continue to grow me spiritually. To this day I remember talks, prayers, sermons, etc. that have and will always leave a lasting impression on me.

To Daniel Shaw, thank you for being there to encourage, inspire, and teach me in so many ways.

You are truly are a great friend and business partner.

To Jay Veal, thanks for all you have done for me while I was in TX. Your business acumen truly is nothing short of amazing and has rubbed off on me in certain areas.

To Ivy N. McQuain thank you for always supporting me regardless of the business venture or circumstance.

To the BLI Group, thank you for publishing this book for me. You have no idea how appreciative I am.

To my readers, thank you for supporting this book and others to come. ☺

Chanelle A. Watson

Encourage
[en- kur –ij, - kuhr -]

verb (used with object) en-cour-aged,

en-cour-ag-ing

"to inspire with courage, spirit, or confidence:"

Press Forward

As a calendar keeps track of time through days,
weeks, months & years
We keep track of our lives through goals,
accomplishments, weaknesses & strengths.

With DAYS, there are new beginnings and
GOALS to set

With WEEKS, there is room for increase with
ACCOMPLISHMENTS to achieve

MONTHS, cause reflection, a means to turn our
WEAKNESSES into STRENGTHS

YEARS, bring about new opportunities to break a
cycle BUT continue to PRESS FORWARD

Press forward in LIFE, press forward in LOVE,
press forward in FAMILY, press forward in
BUSINESS…

Business is the cornerstone to our success, it is a
way to build our dreams and guide our visions

We will encounter DAYS when we struggle to stay
motivated,
WEEKS when it seems like what we do is not
enough, or
MONTHS that add up to YEARS that we do not
see results BUT
we must PRESS FORWARD

Press forward with AMBITION, press forward
with DETERMINATION, press forward in
CONFIDENCE, press forward to ATTACK.

Attack our fears, misconceptions or stumbling
blocks. Attack what's holding us back from
PROGRESS.

Progress that will only come if we PRESS
FORWARD

Press forward with PASSION, press forward with
FOCUS, press forward with FAITH, press forward
with a PURPOSE…

Whatever it takes regardless of the circumstance,
we must always remember to PRESS FORWARD

Are You Made?

Created in His image being Made is the epitome of success

From his walk to his talk, his presence is felt
From her image to her drive, her purpose is seen

With the dimple in his tie and the slit in her dress,
truly being MADE is something that is genderless.

It is a mindset that goes BEYOND prosperity and
reaches HIGHER than the average may possess.

Are you Made?

Putting in work and being dedicated to the vision
Seeing a dream manifest to uphold your destiny
and life's precision

Are you Made?

M - Made to succeed beyond what is visually seen
A – Accomplished enough to know that there is
always room to grow

D – Determined to help others even when you've reached your peak
E – Earn more than money, but respect from your team

Whether man or woman, being Made is a behavior, an attitude, a mentality, a personality, an understanding

It is something that has to be maintained with drive, support, and a strong foundation

Be WILLING to learn and GUIDE those around you
Being ABLE to lead but KNOWING exactly when to follow

That is being Made. That is you. That is me.
BUT only if we continue to strive to achieve

Hidden

Covered by my shadows of doubt,

Disguised by my insecurities

I am Hidden….

My heart becomes a mystery to even me

I have become masked by who people think I
should be

Guarded, by my fears

Only to be unveiled by the King

I WAS Hidden…

I played it safe not wanting to step on people's toes

Not knowing I was being called to have more
confidence,
being given more room to grow

Not knowing my worth, allowed others to treat me
haphazardly

Not being aware of the gem I am, only delayed
God from purifying me,
using ME,
to give Him,
ALL the Glory

I WAS Hidden…

He covered me from circumstances until He
thoroughly pruned my negative surroundings

As I slowly blossom into who I am purposed to be

Now, I am ready

It is my time to conquer who was holding me
back…

ME!

A Dreamer's Reality

I did not raise you to have to live this way?

Son, shouldn't you have graduated by now?

You're my homie and all but, did you really think
they were going to hire you?

Girl, I am married and just had my second child,
when are you going to settle down and find
yourself a husband?

I constantly hear you saying these things,
believing with all your heart you are encouraging,
trying to set certain standards, or just keeping it
real with me

BUT you're NOT

Truth is, YOUR dream FOR ME, is NOT MY
reality

Mom, I love you and you may not have raised me
to live this way BUT,

what you may want for me is not where I am
DESTINED to be.

Dad, I haven't graduated yet because I want my
Master's degree.
The standards I have set for myself are far beyond
the levels you THINK I am able to reach

My "friend", you think you're keeping it real but
please work on your delivery,
Did it ever cross your mind I didn't want to work
for them because they were not good enough for
ME?
My worth would NOT have been appreciated.
Shoot, my growth would have been stagnant,
damn near obsolete

Girl, where you see me not settled because I am
not married with kids,
I see a life devoted to Christ, my faith being
grown, a season of rebuilding, and preparation for
my future husband BECAUSE

"HE who FINDS a wife, finds a good thing…"
NOT searching for a man just to have a ring.

Truth is, YOUR dream FOR ME, is NOT MY
reality

What's Next?

My palms are sweaty as I place this cold blade
against my flesh

I sit here and contemplate what to do as pictures of
my life invade my mind

Visions of playing with my loved ones dance into
my memory, the fun we had penetrates my present

BUT that happiness I FELT is NOTHING like the
PAIN I am feeling NOW.

NOW, I am in school with no direction or plan for
my future

NOW, I am working and HATING every minute

NOW, I have images of a stillborn burned into my
mind

NOW, I am 17 AND pregnant

NOW, I have the smell of the homeless shelter
FOLLOWING ME into every room I enter

NOW, my spouse has left me STRUGGLING to make ends meet, STRUGGLING to raise our children, STRUGGLING with my heart NOW that it's been broken

NOW, I have cancer

Now,

I don't see a reason for living

As my hands begin to shake, this cold blade is pressed DEEPER into my flesh

What's Next?

As a red stream of pain, struggle, defeat, anger, confusion, hurt… slowly trickles onto the floor a Voice so faint invades my Heart, my Soul, my Mind

My child, do not let TEMPORARY moments of pain turn into a PERMANENT moment you can NEVER take back

"...Do not fear, for I am with you; do not be dismayed, for I am your God, I will strengthen you and help you; I will uphold you with my righteous right hand"
(Isaiah 41:10 NIV)

This Voice became louder, this Voice began to penetrate my mouth, this Voice began to sound like mine

"Cast your cares on the LORD and he will sustain you; he will never let the righteous be shaken"
(Psalm 55:22 NIV)

"Yea, though I walk through the valley of the shadow of death, I will fear no evil; for thou art with me; thy rod and thy staff they comfort me"
(Psalm 23:4 KJV)

"For I know the plans I have for you," says the Lord. "They are plans for good and not for disaster, to give you a future, and a hope"
(Jeremiah 29:11 NLT)

As scriptures began to flow from my mouth, my Spirit became uplifted, my Soul became still, my Mind became clear

My pain did not subside BUT GOD made my vision clear, His Word gave me peace in my time of trouble; His Word gave me STRENGTH to FIGHT!

Keep Going

Runners take your marks…

Get Ready….

Set…

Go!

As my feet hit the ground, and the Wind blows around my body, I look around me to see who I am racing.

I look to my left and see my Fears;
I look to my right and see my Doubts.

I pick up speed,
I look behind and see my Past,
I look in front and see my Destiny.

As I continue to run toward my Destiny the Wind becomes more forceful pushing me forward but, something is pulling at my legs.

I look down and see Trials pulling at my left and Tribulations pulling at my right

I want to stop, the additional weight…unbearable BUT,

I will not let these things consume me; my Future looks so Bright

I KEEP GOING

I keep running… I pass my Failures; I pass my Mistakes.

As the Wind becomes even more forceful and I look forward at my Destiny my arms become heavy.

I look at my left and see my Burdens;
I look at my right and see my Strongholds,
on my shoulders rest the World

Again, I want to stop. I am being suffocated and losing my breath BUT,

Something inside is telling me not to give up so,

I KEEP GOING

The closer I get to my Destiny, the heavier my
body feels,

The closer I get to my Destiny the more obstacles
on the road I face

I jump over Heartache and Abuse

I dodge Financial Stress and Bad Health

As sweat vigorously pours down my face, the
Wind not only pushes me but,

Gives me Strength

I KEEP GOING

As my Destiny gets closer, there is a divide in the
road with two finish lines,

I hear CHEERING on the right with a sense of
warmth, happiness and accomplishment

I hear CLAPPING on the left with a sense of uncertainty, demise, and false security

Lord, which way do I go? Which way will bring me into My Purpose?

As soon as the word Purpose leaves my lips, the Wind that has been following me pulls me to the right

At that moment, my load becomes manageable.

I begin to lose doubt, fear, and my past.

My legs become lighter: trials and tribulations are broken

As the Wind continues to blow, my arms began to move with more force and the cheering increases.

I keep going and my burdens and strongholds are healed, the world on my shoulders is replaced with Life

As the finish line marked Destiny is close enough to touch

Those cheers become faces on the other side of the line.

I see family, I see friends, I see my children and spouse

I see my Dreams becoming a Reality

I look back one last time and see all the negative I had left behind

I glance to my left and see that those claps were chains labeled destruction, despair, and downfall.

I KEEP GOING and follow the Wind

I run directly into my Destiny, into my Purpose, into the path that was created just for Me!

It Was You...

When all seemed like it would go wrong

You were there...

It was You who brought people into my life to intercede for me

It was You who allowed people to encourage me

It was You who allowed life's lessons to teach and humble me

You were there through it ALL

It was You who saw my potential even when I was not even close to it

When I was down on my luck it was You who continually prepared me for the Plan You ordained just for me

You were there through it ALL

There were many moments, days, even years,
when I veered off my yellow brick road BUT

You planted people, situations, Saints, all in my
direction with hopes of steering me to my destiny

You allowed tests to be administered at different
angles; to be sure my Faith was not tainted

It was You... You were there through it ALL

And I thank You!

I thank You for trusting me enough, even when I
didn't trust myself

I thank You for never leaving me, even when I
may have left You momentarily

You were there through it ALL... Thank You!

Awakening Your Heart

"In life there are many times when we close off ourselves to loving again because we have been hurt in the past. To those who have learned to embrace love through the pain I applaud and admire you. To those who have been hurt and may be hesitant to love again, I encourage you to awaken your heart"

~ Chanelle

The Awakening (Part 1)

As the layers of your love begin to penetrate the
invisible wall guarding my heart I begin to
awaken.

The love you show has activated feelings in me
that have been buried.

A fire has been ignited that has been smoldered for
so long,
placing a hold on the layers of hurt, pain,
dishonesty, and uncertainty that have been thrown
on the path that once led to my heart.

I am alive in ways I could not imagine. You have
awakened a side of me that I never knew existed.

Now that you have dug a tunnel to my heart, what
will you do with this new awakening?

To be continued ...

Forbidden Fruit

I reflect on the whirlwind of emotions that only
you have stirred in me.
These emotions unparalleled to anything I have
experienced before.

A sense of urgency, transparency, impatience, fear,
passion, nervousness, and enchantment fill me.

As I long to spend physical time with you, be in
your personal space and presence, I encounter an
unfulfilled mission to slowly develop the intimacy
of our personal friendship.

I want to be in your embrace and feel your strong
hands hold me. I want to kiss and gently suck on
your soft lips and have our tongues dance and
juices meet.

I want to inhale you, be intoxicated by your scent.
I want to indulge in you.

My Forbidden Fruit…

I want to savor what makes you, you. From what frustrates you to what brings you the most joy. I linger on every encounter, every story, every conversation.

Your image, intelligence, spirit, humor, strength, and nurturing ability entice me and I become awestruck.

This fruit I encounter daily is still an enigma to me, an untold story that inhabits my thoughts with ease.

This fruit illuminates wants and desires in me that are not easily attainable, there is still more missing, more to experience, more to learn.

Questions mount inside me.
Will I receive an opportunity to experience your true presence?
Why do I feel this way?
Why do I want so much from this season and in the back of my mind know it could never be?
Why do I want to run but still stay?

Will I ever be able to peel away your layers until I
reach your sweetness?
Will I ever be able to taste your imperfections?

My Forbidden Fruit...

Confusion takes a lead in all my emotions. Being
unbalanced and allured by this fruit scares me.

Not wanting to settle for a portion of this fruit but
wanting to just partake in whatever is slowly
revealed causes an internal battle. Wanting this
person...you...my forbidden fruit, to see my spirit
but desiring for you to penetrate my inner desires.

You...my forbidden fruit are so perfect for me but
so imperfect for me, and that draws me closer

You...are a mystery.

You...hypnotize me.

You...

My Forbidden Fruit

The Last Time

As I sit here waiting to hear from you,
My heartbeat is so rapid; my chest feels like it will
explode

The last time we spoke, you were rushing,
The last time I read your words, we were not on
good terms
The last time I saw your face we were silent, only
a hug and a brief call as I departed

As all these last times bombard my mind, I hope
our last time does not end like that

I want our last moments to be filled with love,
compassion, kind words, positivity, support,
encouragement
I want our last moments to reflect how much we
care about each other
I want our last moments… scratch that I just want
to build more moments

I want more moments to be in your presence and
more moments to express how much I love and
care for you
I want to know that you are all right
I want to hear your smile and feel your heartbeat
I want you

As I sit hear waiting to hear from you,
My heartbeat is so rapid; my chest feels like it will
explode

I pray that it is not our last time…

I pray we still can build more moments

Traces of You

A single tear kisses my cheek and leaves TRACES
OF YOU behind
My heart shatters into unrecognizable pieces with
memories of you and plans for us

As I think of what we could have been, I realize
we never were
My imagination must have gotten the best of me,
pulling me in a direction FAR from reality

Nights with me dreaming of being in your arms
Daydreams of kissing you and praying nothing
would go wrong
Our intimacy, without physically being ONE,
made love to me

With every touch, every laugh, every story, every
glimpse of your dreams and visions,
your passions and your heart spoke to me

It spoke to me in a way only I could understand, in
a way that the idea of an "us" felt just right.

Or could this reality be just one of my many
fantasies of you and me?

As a single tear develops into a stream, then into a
river flowing down my face, TRACES OF YOU
are left behind

My tears representing my love for you, and my
hopes and desires for US
You my motivation, you my love, you, the one
who could be my everything

As my tears flow endlessly down my cheeks
TRACES OF YOU are left behind

You, my inspiration, my support, my true love
Or so I thought

Every King needs a Queen and I was ready to put
on the crown that honored your name
Hold the staff that increased your support
And wear the gloves that protected your heart

The love I have for you, words could truly never
express but the affection I possess is felt
nonetheless

As I wipe the TRACES OF YOU from my cheeks,
I wonder if there will ever be
But at this point only God knows if my thoughts
ever were a reality

Until then,

A single tear kisses my cheek and leaves TRACES
OF YOU behind

You Have My Heart: The Awakening (Part II)

As minutes passed, hours grew, and days
multiplied so did my love for you.

Our peak of love, learning, and building

Blossomed into trials and tribulations

My heart left broken, yet again.

Part of me is telling myself never to open up to this
pain again,
the other part of me longs to keep from applying
additional layers of fear for someone else to knock
down to reach my core,

My focus needs to change…

Instead of wanting to build a relationship with him,
my focus became Him

Where doubt & worrying used to consume me,
Prayer & Faith have grown me

The areas I wanted to focus on changing about you, God changed in me

My new journey has begun...

Not only has my heart been awakened but so has my Life…

God will show me who to expose my heart to, I just have to be open & trust

Lord, You have my heart.

My awakening, now has truly just begun…

When Love Waits

There are many ways to love me and you choose
the ways that I've never seen

Your focus isn't my body but the true essence of
my being

You encourage me to do better and treat me like
your Queen

When I'm at my weakest moments, your love lifts
me

Our love goes beyond what either holds in between
our...

Legs, which we use to support each other because
we are team

It is not "I" but "We" who have a dream to focus
on God and build our love with Him as the
foundation

When Love waits in one area it manifests stronger in others

When Love waits all emotions are experienced and felt

When Love waits the heart heals, grows, and connects to whom it's meant for

Our love will last because we built a bond more durable than anything either of us has ever seen.

So when two finally become one we won't have far to go because we already became one mentally.

In His Time

To My Future Love,

I think of you often, pray for you regularly,
prepare for you daily

Wondering if we've already crossed paths or
if God is hiding us from each other,
our moment not being right

The invisible force of our Creator connecting us
from the start
builds great anticipation and trust in His timing,
He made us specifically for each other
Our God knows our hearts

When I close my eyes your smell fills the air,
a smell so familiar
but one that has yet to penetrate my atmosphere

Questions begin to flood my mind
Who?
What?
Where?

When?
How?
Ha… Why?
When I know at the end of the day it will happen,
in His time

Your embrace so passionate, our Faith so strong
Our God knows what we NEED
In addition to what I may want

The love we have for each other creates euphoria
and with God as our foundation
we will never go wrong

We are meant to be
There is no doubt in my mind
The only thing we have to do is be ready

In His time

"Perfect" Formation

Your chocolate brown eyes penetrate my soul
leaving all crevices untouched,
my deepest desires exposed.

Your lips, soft, and sweet as they press against
mine cause my body to melt in your gentle yet firm
embrace.

This Godly Man who has redeveloped in front of
me holds no limits to my heart's happiness.

With every word of encouragement, guidance,
inspiration, scripture, listening ear, my love grows
deeper Spiritually, Mentally, Physically,
Emotionally, yet to cross the boundaries of
Sexually.

As our bodies become One our Spirits intertwine
and form the perfect creation. God giving our
Hearts to each other, you Leading, me Following,
and US Surrendering to Him.

With Our Father as the foundation, and US seeing
God in each other with no wanting to stray,
the strength we possess as One flesh will never be
defeated.
For our three, mirror, God in three and we are
equally yoked in His Spirit.

For your missing rib is returned and a life in Christ
will be presented in "Perfect" Formation.

When God Speaks...

When God Speaks,
It is our choice to listen
But following Him should be our life's mission

A Voice so Powerful yet so subtle
when He needs us to pay close attention
is in tune with our hearts through His Spirit, our
Redemption

Will we hear Him over our thoughts
even if our plan is something different?

His focus not only on our future,
But preparing and molding us to walk directly into
it

When God Speaks,
Trust and Faith are simultaneous
Healing can happen in an instant.

A relationship with the Creator exceeds beyond
levels we even knew existed

When God Speaks,
It is our choice to listen
But following Him is our life's mission

 Eternity

[ih-tur-ni-tee]
- noun, plural e-ter-ni-ties

1. "infinite time; duration without beginning or end"
2. "eternal existence, especially as contrasted with mortal life: the eternity of God"
3. "the timeless state into which the soul passes at a person's death"

~~~~~~~~

Even with multiple definitions, there is only One
who gives Life to an Eternity
God; the Father, the Son & the Holy Spirit
The Holy Trinity

Created in His image,
our purpose,
live for Him while building His Kingdom

Let Go and Let God,
Give it All to Him,

Let Him Mold Us & Shape Us,
Trust in His Plan
Are phrases infused into us as we travel along our
Spiritual Journey
To remind us that Eternity is with Him

"For God so loved the world, that he gave his only
Son, that whoever believes in him should not
perish but have eternal life." (John 3:16 ESV)

When times get hard
do not worry, PRAY

When you feel like you cannot go on anymore,
do not give up, God is your STRENGTH

Some people spend their lives trying to find the
way, trying to be rich, longing for success when
it's not about us, but about Him

Some think when we take our last breath that is the
end,
I'm here to tell you that at that moment, that if you
lived for God, Life just begins

Eternity

"…if you confess with your mouth that Jesus is Lord and believe in your heart that God raised him from the dead, you will be saved."
(Romans 10:9 ESV)

APPENDIX:

Author's Commentary: Moment of Reflection

While writing this book, I had continual moments of prayer and reflection on places I have been in my life journey and things I have witnessed. For each poem I have written there is a story, there is an emotion I wanted to reveal, there are instances where I wanted to uncover topics that society does not often mention or may desensitize. Not only do I want whoever is reading to relate to the poems, regardless of gender, I want them to be inspired to follow their own dreams, or encourage someone else. Through each poem and the order they are placed in the book, I wanted a story to be told. There are seven poems geared to encouraging and inspiring and ten focused on awakening the Heart/Spirit, the number seven representing God's perfect number and the number 10 symbolizing completion. Here are my thoughts on each poem.

Press Forward

In life we all have goals that we set for ourselves, we all go through struggles, setbacks or redirect our lives based on what has been thrown at us. Within this poem I wanted to focus on encouraging ours and myself to always press forward. Regardless if we do not see all of what we are doing manifest itself right then and there we must continue to strive for those goals.

Are You Made?

A lot of times I think as a society we focus on success as having money, cars, clothes, etc. and with this poem, I wanted to give a different interpretation of what being made and being successful can be. Even if we do not have a whole lot of money but we have direction, are following our purpose, and are able to help and encourage others along the way then we are made, we are successful, we have accomplished a goal that not many can say they have. I strongly believe we gain respect from other's not because of the amount of success or money we may have but because even with those things we are still there to help, encourage or inspire someone else to grow and reach their peak. Being made to me is a continual cycle of uplifting and helping others.

Hidden

Hidden is about how in our lives there are moments when we don't know our own identities, how we are still trying to find ourselves while being around people who know exactly where they are going in their lives. How we may hide from the "spotlight" because we don't understand it or what it may entail when in fact that is where we are meant to be. We may be hiding ourselves when God wants us to be seen because we were created to make a difference in people's lives. This poem is a glimpse of how having self-love and self-worth can change how you view life and how we can go from being hidden to embracing our worth and direction to make a different in the world around us.

A Dreamer's Reality

Often times in our lives not only do we have a dream of what we imagine are lives to be like but so do our families or friends. They envision how we should live our lives based on their terms or what they may or may not have accomplished for themselves. *A Dreamer's Reality* is a play on these people in our lives that we love but bring us down spiritually, mentally, or even emotionally. It is meant to encourage anyone in this situation to know it is ok to live his or her life on your own terms. That someone else's dreams may not be our reality. What we vision has nothing to do with them but ourselves.

What's Next?

I wrote this poem to shed light on suicide being a disease. You never know who may be going through these emotions sometimes until it is too late. We never know why someone may want to end his or her lives, what he or she may be going through and I wanted this poem to encourage anyone going through these emotions, anyone who has experienced or witnessed someone going through these emotions, to be encouraged to keep going and know that God has the final say. To know that God created each of us with a purpose in mind that regardless of any struggles we have endured, regardless if our thoughts and plans for ourselves are not manifesting that does not mean that God is not using us for a greater good.

Keep Going

Keep Going is one of my favorite poems. I remember the day I wrote this poem and didn't know if it got the message I wanted to get across clear enough, or if it was too long and would lose the reader's attention but when I had a close friend of mine read it aloud to me, the way he read it truly brought life to what I was trying to get across.

I placed it after *What's Next?* because I feel like it answers the question of *What's Next?* for many people regardless of their situation or state of mind. We must *Keep Going* because that next step we take, especially when going through a situation, can be our breakthrough into what God has called us for. That next step we take can place us back on track to accomplishing the goals that we have set for ourselves and be in line with the plan God has mapped out for us.

There are many words that I capitalize to offer personification. I wanted the Wind in the poem to personify God because though He is so very Powerful when we are going through something He can be just as subtle as wind moving us from going in the wrong direction or continuing in the direction we are going, even if it does not seem right. I capitalized Fear, Tribulations, Doubts, Struggles, etc. because though they are lifeless words we give them life when we focus too much on them. We give these words more power than we should at times, these words personified correlate with the adversary because it plants those seeds in our minds.

I also wanted the poem to embody a race because in life there are many times when we feel like we are competing against this woman or man to get a job, get married, get the man/woman we are attracted to but in fact we are really competing against ourselves. We hold ourselves back, we are always going to be our worst critics so in the poem instead of battling or racing against someone else the runner is in a race with their past, their thoughts, anything that is trying to hold them back from what God has for them. At the end of the race and throughout the race as they keep going they see that they are victorious and that God has been there all along.

It was You...

This poem is an open letter to God from myself. I have been on a very interesting journey throughout my life and have experienced so many people, some many environments, so many things that have shaped me into the woman I have become and I know that is only because of God's doing. I know I have probably veered off of the path He originally had for me but God always gets what He wants and gives us what we need, and gets us back on track. He is truly ALWAYS there. ☺

~~~~~~~~~

The Awakening (Part I)

This is the first poem in the section for *Awakening Your Heart* so I wanted it to show growth. The layers of all struggles, past relationship etc. have been lifted and now it is time to love wholeheartedly, with no limitations. A new beginning has been ignited and the first couple of poems that follow are the journey through love that we all take.

Forbidden Fruit

This is another one of my long poems but one that is close to my heart because we all have that person who we consider to be our *Forbidden Fruit*. The person who first popped into our head when we read the poem, the person who if they call you, the good, the bad, and the ugly all race into your mind at one time. This poem is an ode to our *Forbidden Fruits*.

The Last Time

This poem just focuses on how sometimes we can let life get to us. Whether it's with a loved one, a friend or a significant other there are times we tend to let our emotions get the best of us. There are times we may let feuds go on for years to then find out that the person who we may have been feuding with is now ill or worse. I wanted this poem to embody those feelings and emotions. And possibly encourage whoever reads it to create new moments with the person(s) in their life.

Traces of You

This poem stemmed from a situation I was going through. As women there are times we try to make things work even if they are not or were not supposed to work. Sometimes our love or wanting for something overpowers what is actually going on in a relationship until it all hits us like a ton of bricks and we are left with a broken heart. With this poem I wanted every thought, every tear to express healing so even though we are hurt and going through, we are giving ourselves that moment to realize what the situation was and heal during the process.

You Have My Heart: The Awakening (Part II)

At this point, we see the journey that has developed from *The Awakening: (Part I)*. This poem picks up where the other one left off in a sense that now we realized that after it all started great it has again ended like before but what's different about this time is that our focus has changed from a relationship with a man/woman to having a relationship with God and having Him prepare and lead us to who He has for us.

When Love Waits

Love has many meanings but in this poem I wanted it to represent love sexually and non-sexually and how both can exist in a relationship. Often times we focus so much on the sexual that we may mistake that for love or think that is all love entails, when there is more to loving someone than just being sexually intimate. I wanted this poem to show that love has many forms.

In His Time

This poem is written as a letter to the reader's future mate. It shows what happens after we let

God be in control and allow the person who He had for us to enter our lives, *In His Time*.

When God Speaks

There are many times *When God Speaks* and we may not listen in the beginning but as our relationship grows with Him that hesitation or confusion of whether it is Him or ourselves diminishes. This poem illustrates that growth, that relationship with Him, and being able to know when God speaks and hearing him even beyond our own thoughts.

"Perfect" Formation

This poem illustrates the ending of one journey and the beginning of another. Our heart has now been awakened and new love has been found. The difference between this love and the love we thought was represented in *"The Awakening (Part I)"* is that God is the foundation to this new love we have found.

Eternity

The title of this book is *From My Heart To Your Soul: A Collection of Poetry To Encourage, Inspire and Awaken YOUR Spirit*, so to me it was only right to have the tenth poem (God's number of completion) in the section geared toward awakening your heart be focused on giving our lives to God and focusing on the *Eternity* that comes only if we live for Him. This poem is my way to complete the book and bring it full circle so that not only were you encouraged, and inspired but your Spirit was awakened.

PAST, PRESENT, FUTURE:
Excerpt from *The Confidant*

As I sit there and listen to their stories a thick dark cloud enters the room. Breathing becomes a struggle.

YOU DON'T KNOW WHAT I'VE BEEN THROUGH, they yell at each other in unison.

"Every night I thought of ways to protect my mother, sister, and myself from my father who was always ready to attack after coming from the bar," she exclaimed.

"My mother left me when I was 4, and I had to stay with my aunt whose boyfriend would molest me," he yelled as tears slowly trickled down his cheeks.

As they went tit for tat trying to outdo each other with the struggles they have experienced and survived throughout the years, light began to shine. The anger for one another for not understanding turned into empathy, remorse, closure and healing.

As the room began to let in more light, the healing continued.

It was not the fact they had a past, which they hid from each other until this day. It was the fact they were letting their past interfere with their present, blocking their future together.

CREDITS

The Holy Bible is the source for all biblical scriptures referenced throughout the book and within the poems. The author used the King James Version (KJV), the English Standard Version (ESV), the New International Version (NIV), and New Living Translation (NLT) of the Holy Bible to ensure that each scripture flowed with the poem and can be understood by the reader. All translations used were not modified beyond their translation.

In reference to the definitions used throughout the book, the author used Dictionary.com.

INDEX

ABOUT THE AUTHOR

Chanelle was born and raised in New York and attended the University of New Haven in West Haven, CT. Upon completion in 2004 she earned a Bachelor of Science degree in Criminal Justice with a concentration in Investigative Services, a Bachelor of Science in Legal Studies with a concentration in Public Affairs, as well a Paralegal Certificate.

Her love and PASSION for baking and cooking superseded working in the Criminal Justice field and she moved to the Dallas, TX area in 2010 to attend the Art Institute of Dallas with the goal of honing her skills of cooking and desiring to start her own restaurant. Hence, she has started Chanelle's Heavenly Treasures, a premiere dessert and catering business currently serving the New York Tri-State area (NY, CT, NJ) and shipping to select U.S.

In Chanelle's spare time she also has a great passion for reading and writing. These passions birthed her first published book *From My Heart to Your Eyes* with cookbooks, and children's books to soon follow.

Chanelle Watson
Author
info@chanelleawatson.com
www.chanelleawatson.com
www.facebook.com/ChanelleAWatson

Knee Pain Relief

Exercises & Stretches –

Made in the USA
San Bernardino, CA
26 October 2014